EDWARD ELGAR

INTRODUCTION AND ALLEGRO

for Strings
Op. 47

D1293432

Ernst Eulenburg Ltd

London · Mainz · Madrid · New York · Paris · Tokyo · Toronto · Zürich

PREFACE/VORWORT

The string orchestra is a medium that has proved particularly attractive to British composers of the twentieth century, drawing masterpieces from, among others, Ralph Vaughan Williams (1872–1958), Benjamin Britten (1913–76) and Michael Tippett (b.1905). The challenge to excel was surely laid down in 1905 with the first performance of Elgar's *Introduction and Allegro*.

The impetus to its composition came in 1904 when members of the recently-formed London Symphony Orchestra asked for a new piece to play at an all-Elgar concert he had agreed to conduct in March 1905. As usual, Elgar consulted his friend August Jaeger (1860–1909), of Novello & Company, who, on 28 October, wrote enthusiastically suggesting 'a *brilliant* quick *string* Scherzo [. . .] you might even write a *modern Fugue* for Strings.'[1] The idea sank in and on 26 January 1905 Elgar announced: 'I'm doing that string thing in time for the Sym. Orch. concert. Intro: & Allegro – no *working-out* part but a devil of a fugue instead.'[2] The piece seems to have been completed on or about 13 February and the performance took place at Queen's Hall on 8 March.

Die britischen Komponisten des 20. Jahrhunderts haben eine besondere Vorliebe für das Streichorchester, das unter anderem Komponisten wie Ralph Vaughan Williams (1872–1958), Benjamin Britten (1913–76) und Michael Tippett (geb. 1905) zur Schaffung von Meisterwerken inspiriert hat. Sicher wurde der Grundstein für die Herausforderung, Hervorragendes zu leisten, mit der ersten Aufführung von Elgars *Introduction and Allegro* gelegt.

Den Anstoß zu dieser Komposition hatten 1904 Mitglieder des erst kurz zuvor gegründeten London Symphony Orchestra gegeben, die um ein neues Stück baten, das bei einem ausschließlich der Musik Elgars gewidmeten und von ihm selbst zu dirigierenden Konzert im März des Jahres 1905 vorgetragen werden sollte. Wie gewöhnlich zog Elgar zunächst einmal seinen Freund August Jaeger (1860–1909) vom Novello-Verlag zu Rate, der ihm in seinem Brief vom 28. Oktober daruufhin voller Begeisterung ,,ein *brillantes*, schnelles *Streicher*-Scherzo'' vorschlug, ja er könne ,,sogar eine *moderne Fuge* für Streicher schreiben''[1]. Die Idee fiel bei Elgar auf fruchtbaren Boden, und am 26. Januar 1905 verkündete er: ,,Diese Streichersache wird rechtzeitig zum Konzert des Symphony Orchestra fertig. Intro: & Allegro – jedoch kein *Themenverarbeitungsteil*, sondern statt dessen eine grandiose Fuge''[2]. Beendet hat er das Stück offenbar am oder um den 13. Februar herum. Zur Aufführung kam es dann am 8. März in der Queen's Hall.

[1] Jerrold Northrop Moore, *Edward Elgar – A Creative Life*, London 1984, p.451
[2] Percy M. Young, *Letters from Nimrod to Edward Elgar*, London 1965, pp.248-9

[1] Jerrold Northrop Moore, *Edward Elgar – A Creative Life*, London 1984, S. 451
[2] Percy M. Young, *Letters from Nimrod to Edward Elgar*, London 1965, S. 248f.

IV

Despite Lady Elgar's excited verdict 'Many people think it the finest thing he has written [. . .]',[3] critical reception was cool and remained so even after a second performance on 19 March. It may well be that the orchestra, fine as it was, was as yet unable to do justice to the virtuoso string writing (still a considerable challenge!). In time, however, the work came to be recognized for what it is – a masterpiece.

Although the formal structure of the *Introduction and Allegro* makes a reference to traditional practices, its most striking feature is its waywardness. The themes grow freely out of each other, gradually creating a natural form that is only distantly related to the classical sonata movement. In its use of a string quartet as well as massed strings the work has something in common with the concerto grosso, though the alternation between solo and ripieno players is never carried out in true baroque fashion. The 58-bar Introduction (*Moderato*) presents four themes in quick succession: an opening fanfare of downward fourths; a rising figure (bar 5, *Allegretto poco stringendo*) given out by the quartet and immediately taken up by the whole orchestra; a countersubject to the rising figure, heard first in the lower strings (bar 7, *Moderato*); and finally, a melancholy tune built on thirds, played first by the solo viola (bar 18). This tune is an elaboration of an idea that came to Elgar in 1901 during a holiday in Wales and which, during the gestation of the *Introduction and Allegro*, he recalled on hearing a distant voice singing in the Wye valley near his Herefordshire

Auch wenn Lady Elgar voller Begeisterung zu dem Werk anmerkte: ,,Viele Leute halten es für das Beste, was er je geschrieben hat"[3], so wurde es von den Kritikern doch eher mit Zurückhaltung aufgenommen. Daran änderte sich auch nach seiner erneuten Aufführung am 19. März nichts. Denkbar wäre jedoch, daß das Orchester, ungeachtet seiner Qualitäten, zu besagtem Zeitpunkt einfach noch nicht in der Lage war, dem virtuosen Streicherwerk (auch heute noch eine große Herausforderung) gerecht zu werden. Mit der Zeit erlangte es aber dennoch die ihm gebührende Anerkennung als Meisterwerk.

Obgleich sich die formale Struktur von *Introduction and Allegro* an traditionelle Methoden anlehnt, fällt vor allem seine Eigenwilligkeit ins Auge. Aus einem Thema entwickelt sich zwanglos das nächste, wodurch eine natürliche Satzform geschaffen wird, die nur noch sehr entfernte Bezüge zum klassischen Sonatensatz aufweist. Der Einsatz eines Streichquartetts sowie von geballten Streichern verleiht dem Werk etwas von einem Concerto grosso, wenn auch der Wechsel zwischen Solo- und Ripieno-Spielern niemals in der ursprünglichen, barocken Weise erfolgt. Der aus 58 Takten bestehende Eröffnungssatz (*Moderato*) stellt in rascher Abfolge vier Themen vor: eine Eröffnungsfanfare aus abfallenden Quarten; eine aufsteigende Figur (Takt 5, *Allegretto poco stringendo*), die vom Quartett eingeführt und sogleich vom gesamten Orchester aufgegriffen wird; als drittes ein mit der aufsteigenden Figur kontrastierendes Thema, das zuerst in den unteren Streichern (Takt 7, *Moderato*) zu hören ist; und schließlich eine melancholische, auf Terzen aufbauende Melodie, die zunächst von der Solo-Bratsche (Takt 18) ausgeführt wird.

---

[3] Ibid, p.250

[3] Ibid., S. 250

V

home, Plas Gwyn.[4] It is this theme that brings the introductory section to its quiet end in G minor.

The Allegro section begins at fig. 7 with a G-major version of the Introduction's second theme. A contrasting subject – a bustling semiquaver figure full of nervous energy and subtly based on the general shape of the 'Welsh' tune – appears at fig. 10. This gradually embraces the opening fanfare idea and prepares the way for what in orthodox sonata-form would be a Development section, but which, as Elgar explained, is replaced by a vigorous Fugue. Although the fugue Subject has certain features in common with what has gone before it is, to all intents and purposes, a new idea. A compact recapitulation now follows and the movement ends with a triumphant Coda in which the 'Welsh' tune appears in full glory.

The score first published by Novello and Company carried the inscription, 'to his friend Professor S. S. Sandford, Yale University, USA'.

Michael Hurd

Diese Melodie stellt die Ausarbeitung einer Idee dar, die Elgar 1901 bei einem Besuch in Wales hatte: Während des Reifungsprozesses von *Introduction and Allegro* kam sie ihm wieder ins Gedächtnis, als er im Wye Valley in der Nähe seines Heimatortes Plas Gwyn in Herefordshire in der Ferne jemanden singen hörte[4]. Mit diesem Thema wird der Eröffnungssatz leise in g-Moll beendet.

Der *Allegro*-Satz beginnt bei Ziffer 7 mit einer G-Dur-Variante des II. Themas des Eröffnungssatzes. Bei Ziffer 10 setzt dann ein kontrastierendes Thema, eine quirlige Sechzehntel-Figur voll angespannter Energie, ein, die auf sehr subtile Weise auf der Gesamtform der ,,Walisischen" Weise beruht. Sie schließt allmählich wieder die Fanfarenidee der Eröffnung ein und bereitet den Weg für etwas, was im orthodoxen Sonatensatz ein Durchführungsteil wäre, hier aber – wie Elgar erklärend bemerkt – durch eine dynamische Fuge ersetzt wird. Bestehen auch gewisse Gemeinsamkeiten zwischen Fugen-Thema und dem Vorangegangenen, so handelt es sich doch im Grunde um eine völlig neue Idee. Schließlich folgt eine gedrängte Reprise, worauf der Satz mit einer triumphalen Coda endet, in der die ,,Walisische" Weise in ihrer ganzen Pracht erscheint.

Die von Novello and Company erstveröffentlichte Partitur trägt die Inschrift ,,für seinen Freund Professor S. S. Sandford, Yale University, USA".

Michael Hurd
Übersetzung Gabriele Vogt

[4] Michael Kennedy, *Portrait of Elgar*, London 1968, pp.181-2

[4] Michael Kennedy, *Portrait of Elgar*, London 1968, S. 181f.

From the autograph score
Aus dem Autograph der Partitur

INTRODUCTION AND ALLEGRO

Edward Elgar
(1857–1934)
Op. 47

2

4

14

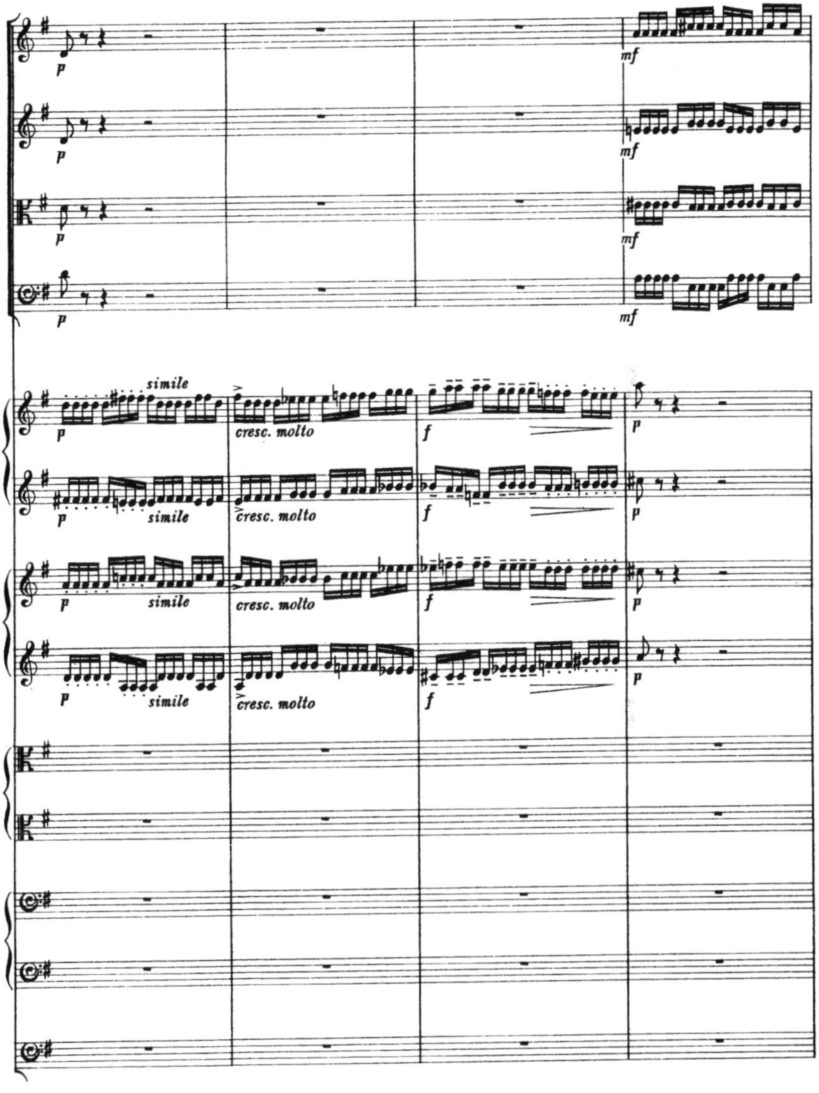
p
mf
simile
cresc. molto
f

11

11

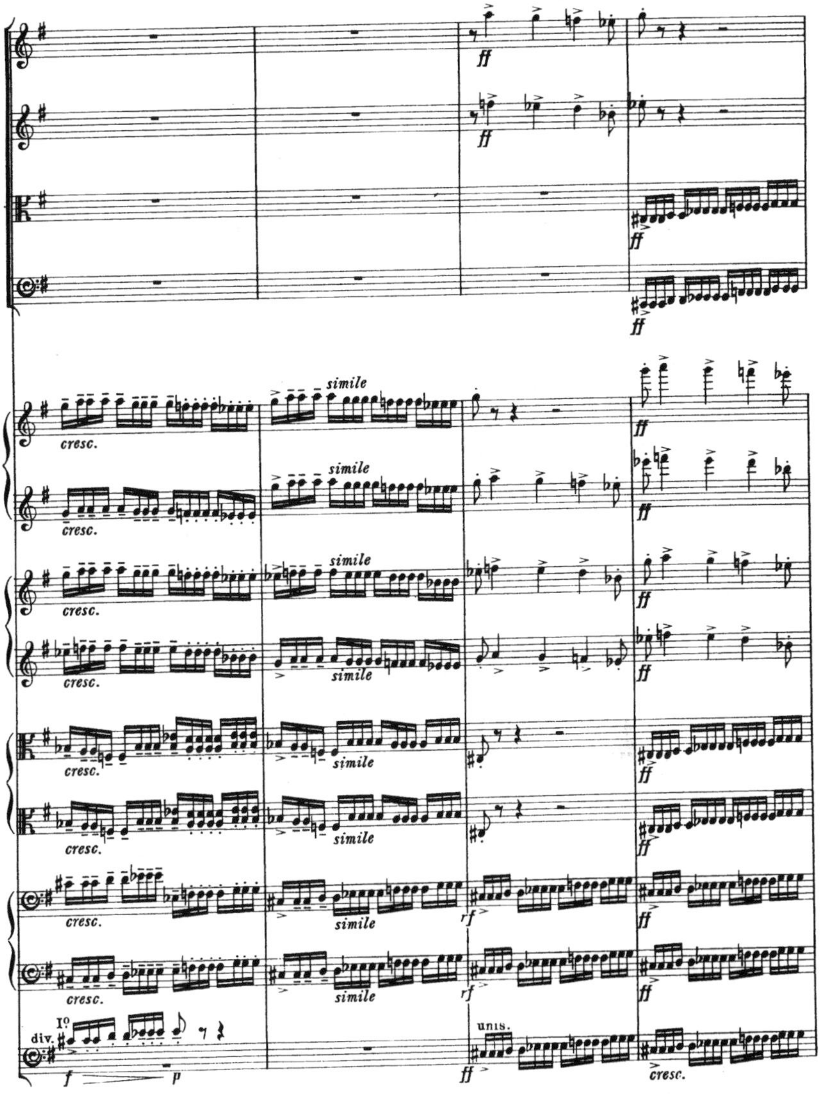
ff
cresc.
simile
rf
I°
div.
unis.
f
p

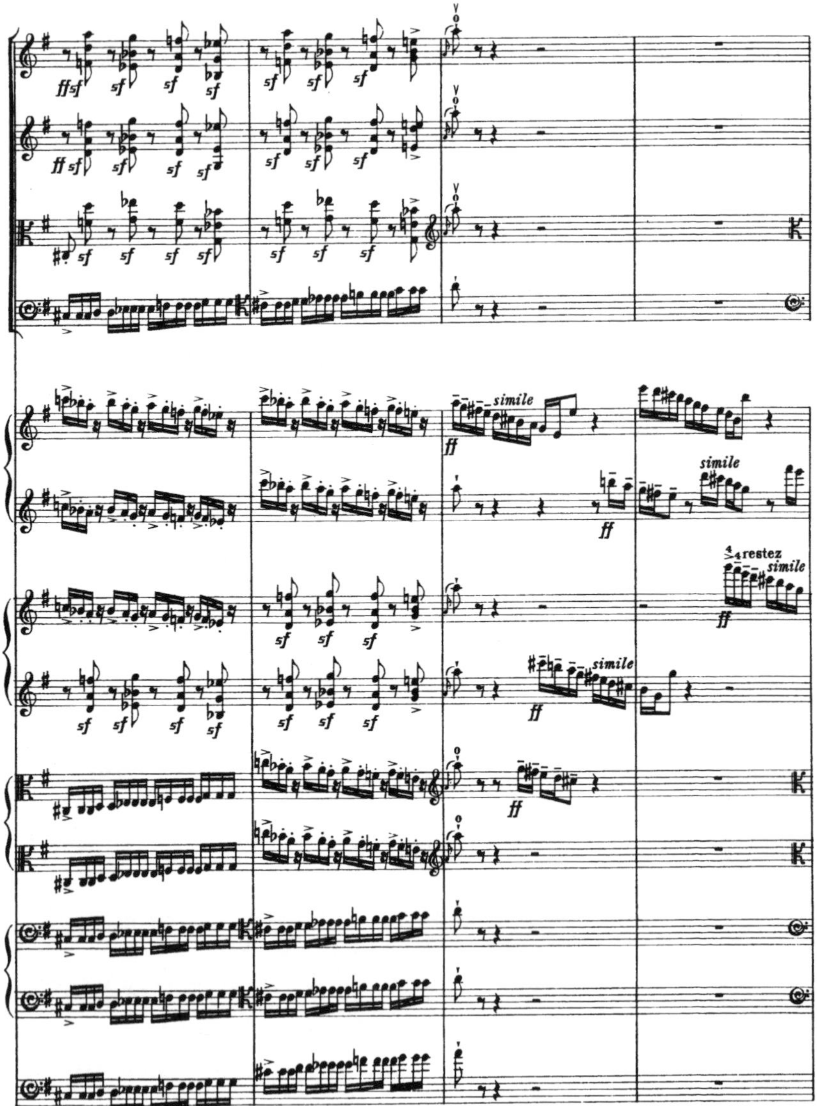
simile
simile
restez
simile
simile

14 brillante, con tutta forza.

26

34

20 poco a poco meno mosso.

42

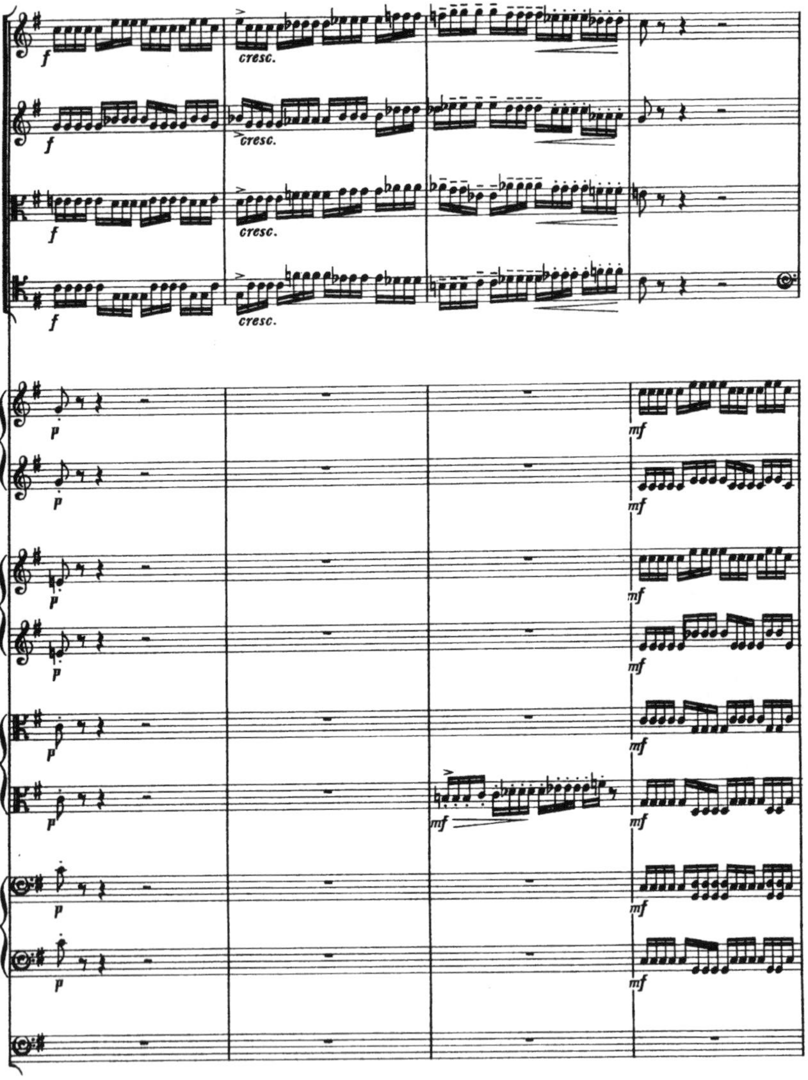
f
cresc.
divisi
p
mf

ff sf
ff sf
ff sf
ff sf
simile
ff
simile
ff
4 restez
simile
ff
simile
ff
ff
simile
ff
simile
ff
simile
ff
simile
ff
ff

56

EE 6767